SERIOUS CONCERNS

Wendy Cope was born in Erith, Kent. She was educated at Farringtons School and subsequently went to St Hilda's College, Oxford, where she learned to play the guitar. After university she worked for fifteen years as a primary-school teacher in London. Her first collection of poems, *Making Cocoa for Kingsley Amis*, was published in 1986. In 1987 she received a Cholmondeley Award for poetry. She is now a freelance writer.

WENDY COPE

Serious Concerns

faber and faber
LONDON·BOSTON

First published in 1992
by Faber and Faber Limited
3 Queen Square London WC1N 3AU

Photoset by Wilmaset Ltd, Wirral
Printed in England by Clays Ltd, St Ives plc
All rights reserved

A CIP record for this book is available from
the British Library

ISBN 0 571 16705 5

6 8 10 9 7

Contents

Acknowledgements

Each of the following newspapers and periodicals has published one or more of these poems: *Author*, *Daily Telegraph*, *Guardian*, *Independent*, *Independent on Sunday*, *Observer*, *Orbis*, *Oxford Poetry*, *Poetry Review*, *Spectator*, *Status*, *Sunday Telegraph* and *Sunday Times*.

'The Concerned Adolescent', 'I Worry' and 'Exchange of Letters' first appeared in Poetry Book Society anthologies, 'Roger Bear's Football Poems' in *Castles on the Ground* (Mary Glasgow, 1989). 'A Christmas Poem' was commissioned by the Canadian Broadcasting Corporation, '19th Christmas Poem' by the *Daily Telegraph*, and 'The Uncertainty of the Poet' by the Tate Gallery for the anthology *With a Poet's Eye* (1986).

'Faint Praise' was first published pseudonymously in the competition section of the *Spectator*.

Some of the poems were published in *Men and Their Boring Arguments* (Wykeham Press, 1988) or in *Does She Like Word-Games?* (Anvil, 1988), both limited-edition booklets.

'Strugnell Lunaire', 'the homeless hammer' (inspired by René Char's 'le marteau sans maître', set to music by Pierre Boulez) and 'Ahead of My Time' (inspired by Karlheinz Stockhausen's 'für kommende Zeiten') are from *Strugnell's Song Cycle*, a work-in-progress. This project was suggested to the author by Colin Matthews, who is collaborating with Strugnell on the music.

I

Bloody Men

Bloody men are like bloody buses –
You wait for about a year
And as soon as one approaches your stop
Two or three others appear.

You look at them flashing their indicators,
Offering you a ride.
You're trying to read the destinations,
You haven't much time to decide.

If you make a mistake, there is no turning back.
Jump off, and you'll stand there and gaze
While the cars and the taxis and lorries go by
And the minutes, the hours, the days.

Flowers

Some men never think of it.
You did. You'd come along
And say you'd nearly brought me flowers
But something had gone wrong.

The shop was closed. Or you had doubts –
The sort that minds like ours
Dream up incessantly. You thought
I might not want your flowers.

It made me smile and hug you then.
Now I can only smile.
But, look, the flowers you nearly brought
Have lasted all this while.

Defining the Problem

I can't forgive you. Even if I could,
You wouldn't pardon me for seeing through you.
And yet I cannot cure myself of love
For what I thought you were before I knew you.

The Aerial

The aerial on this radio broke
A long, long time ago,
When you were just a name to me –
Someone I didn't know.

The man before the man before
Had not yet set his cap
The day a clumsy gesture caused
That slender rod to snap.

Love came along. Love came along.
Then you. And now it's ended.
Tomorrow I shall tidy up
And get the radio mended.

The Orange

At lunchtime I bought a huge orange –
The size of it made us all laugh.
I peeled it and shared it with Robert and Dave –
They got quarters and I had a half.

And that orange, it made me so happy,
As ordinary things often do
Just lately. The shopping. A walk in the park.
This is peace and contentment. It's new.

The rest of the day was quite easy.
I did all the jobs on my list
And enjoyed them and had some time over.
I love you. I'm glad I exist.

Some More Light Verse

You have to try. You see a shrink.
You learn a lot. You read. You think.
You struggle to improve your looks.
You meet some men. You write some books.
You eat good food. You give up junk.
You do not smoke. You don't get drunk.
You take up yoga, walk and swim.
And nothing works. The outlook's grim.
You don't know what to do. You cry.
You're running out of things to try.

You blow your nose. You see the shrink.
You walk. You give up food and drink.
You fall in love. You make a plan.
You struggle to improve your man.
And nothing works. The outlook's grim.
You go to yoga, cry, and swim.
You eat and drink. You give up looks.
You struggle to improve your books.
You cannot see the point. You sigh.
You do not smoke. You have to try.

As Sweet

It's all because we're so alike –
Twin souls, we two.
We smile at the expression, yes,
And know it's true.

I told the shrink. He gave our love
A different name.
But he can call it what he likes –
It's still the same.

I long to see you, hear your voice,
My narcissistic object-choice.

Loss

The day he moved out was terrible –
That evening she went through hell.
His absence wasn't a problem
But the corkscrew had gone as well.

Another Unfortunate Choice

I think I am in love with A. E. Housman,
Which puts me in a worse-than-usual fix.
No woman ever stood a chance with Housman
And he's been dead since 1936.

Valentine

My heart has made its mind up
And I'm afraid it's you.
Whatever you've got lined up,
My heart has made its mind up
And if you can't be signed up
This year, next year will do.
My heart has made its mind up
And I'm afraid it's you.

II

Serious Concerns

'She is witty and unpretentious, which is both her strength and her limitation.' (Robert O'Brien in the *Spectator*, 25.10.86)

I'm going to try and overcome my limitation –
Away with sloth!
Now should I work at being less witty? Or more
    pretentious?
Or both?

'They (Roger McGough and Brian Patten) have something in common with her, in that they all write to amuse.' (Ibid.)

Write to amuse? What an appalling suggestion!
I write to make people anxious and miserable and to
    worsen their indigestion.

An Unusual Cat-Poem

My cat is dead
But I have decided not to make a big
                              tragedy out of it.

A Christmas Poem

At Christmas little children sing and merry bells
    jingle,
The cold winter air makes our hands and faces
    tingle
And happy families go to church and cheerily they
    mingle
And the whole business is unbelievably dreadful, if
    you're single.

The New Regime

Yes, I agree. We'll pull ourselves together.
We eat too much. We're always getting pissed.
It's not a bad idea to find out whether
We like each other sober. Let's resist.
I've got the Perrier and the carrot-grater,
I'll look on a Scotch or a pudding as a crime.
We all have to be sensible sooner or later
But don't let's be sensible all the time.

No more thinking about a second bottle
And saying 'What the hell?' and giving in.
Tomorrow I'll be jogging at full throttle
To make myself successful, rich and thin.
A healthy life's a great rejuvenator
But, God, it's going to be an uphill climb.
We all have to be sensible sooner or later
But don't let's be sensible all the time.

The conversation won't be half as trivial –
You'll hold forth on the issues of the day –
And, when our evenings aren't quite so convivial,
You'll start remembering the things I say.
Oh, see if you can catch the eye of the waiter
And order me a double vodka and lime.
We all have to be sensible sooner or later
But I refuse to be sensible all the time.

Kindness to Animals

This poem was commissioned by the editor of *The Orange Dove of Fiji*, an anthology for the benefit of the World Wide Fund for Nature. It was rejected as unsuitable.

If I went vegetarian
And didn't eat lambs for dinner,
I think I'd be a better person
And also thinner.

But the lamb is not endangered
And at least I can truthfully say
I have never, ever eaten a barn owl,
So perhaps I am OK.

A Green Song

to sing at the bottle-bank

One green bottle,
Drop it in the bank.
Ten green bottles,
What a lot we drank.
Heaps of bottles
And yesterday's a blank
But we'll save the planet,
Tinkle, tinkle, clank!

We've got bottles –
Nice, percussive trash.
Bags of bottles
Cleaned us out of cash.
Empty bottles,
We love to hear them smash
And we'll save the planet,
Tinkle, tinkle, crash!

The Concerned Adolescent

Our planet spins around the sun
in its oval-shaped orbit
like a moth circling a bright, hot, golden-yellow
    lightbulb.

Look at this beautiful, lovely
blue and green and white jewel
shining against the dark black sky.
It is doomed.

On another planet somewhere far away in the
    galaxy
beings are discussing the problems of Earth.
'It is a wonderful world,' says their leader,
'It has roaring oceans filled with many kinds of
    fishes,
It has green meadows bedecked with white and
    yellow flowers,
Its trees have twisting roots and fruitful, abundant
    branches.
But it is doomed.

'The problem with this lovely, beautiful world, you
    see,
Is the inhabitants, known as HUMAN BEINGS.
Human beings will not live in peace and love
and care for the little helpless creatures who share
    the planet with them.

They pollute the world, they kill and eat the
    animals.
Everywhere there is blood and the stench of death.
Human beings make war and hate one another.
They do not understand their young, they reject
    their ideals,
they make them come home early from the disco.
They are doomed.'

Soon a great explosion, a terrible cloud
will wipe out all the life on this planet,
including those people who do not see how
    important my poem is.
They are certainly doomed.

Goldfish Nation

by Jason Strugnell

In the pond
There are no bombs, no guns, no bullets.
There is no property and no television.
The pond is the territory not of humans
But of the goldfish.
He is better than you.

Goldfish play.
They do not work.
They do not set the alarm clock
And get up at half past seven
And get on a crowded commuter train
And go to the office.
They are playful creatures.
Goldfish play.
Their games are non-competitive –
Swimming into a space and twisting,
Looking for another space.
All day long it's like PE
In a progressive infant school.

Goldfish are intelligent.
They answer to their names.
Go out and sprinkle
Just a pinch of fish food
As you call to them

And see them rising from the muddy depths
To greet you. Sunshine. Goldy.
Flipper. Bertrand Russell.
Maharishi. Name your goldfish
After holy men and sages.
It is appropriate.

'Look on the goldfish,' say the Inkuwala,
'And be at peace.'

The Watatooki of Wideawake Bay
Have a different saying:
'He who contemplates the goldfish
Will grow wiser than a frog.'

Albert Eames of Norwood Fish Society
Believes that his goldfish, Lucky,
Is a bringer of good fortune.
'It's a well-known fact,' he says
'That many goldfish owners in South London
'Have won prizes with their Premium Bonds.'

The sex life of the goldfish, it has to be admitted,
Is somewhat less exciting
Than the mating of whales.

The fact is goldfish do not have a sex life.
They breed without physical contact,
Shedding enormous quantities of sperms and eggs
Into the water.

Hundreds and hundreds of sperms are attracted
To each egg
And each one tries to bore its way through the shell
But only one succeeds in doing so.

After fertilization, the egg faces tremendous
    hazards,
Including the danger of being eaten
By the very fish who gave it life.

But some survive. The fry swim. They eat.
They grow. Their scales ripen to gold.
And they play.

Like Buddhists,
Goldfish are disinclined
To get into an argument.
They do not discuss interest rates .
Or debate the ordination of women.
On these matters they seem to have no opinion.
They prefer to play.

Ludic, aureate creatures,
Silently chanting, *Om*,
Gazing at reality with round, unblinking eyes.
Water-angels, glinting in the sunlight.

It's obvious that goldfish are better than people.
Goldfish are better than you.

Roger Bear's Football Poems

Three cheers for Spurs!
They beat Stoke!
Glad I'm a football fan.
Glad I'm a bloke.

*

Who beat Liverpool
Then beat them again?
Tottenham Hotspur –
A bunch of real men.

*

Tottenham lost
And I am sad.
Sometimes it's difficult
Being a lad.

*

Spurs beat Newcastle,
Just like I reckoned.
Spurs are brilliant
And now they are second.

*

Will they beat Everton?
We'll have to see.
Please get a ticket
For Wendy and me.

Roger Bear's Philosophical Pantoum

I stare at the ceiling.
I look very wise.
Up with thinking and feeling
And stuff exercise.

I look very wise –
I am keen on reflection
And stuff. Exercise?
I prefer introspection.

I am keen on reflection,
Like old Aristotle –
I prefer introspection
To hitting the bottle.

Like old Aristotle,
I rarely descend
To hitting the bottle –
My arms will not bend.

I rarely descend
As far as the floor.
My arms will not bend –
Sometimes life is a bore.

As far as the floor –
A long way to fall.
Sometimes life is a bore.
I gaze at the wall.

A long way to fall –
I lie on the quilt.
I gaze at the wall,
I wrestle with guilt.

I lie on the quilt
On my comfortable bed.
I wrestle with guilt
Until I am fed.

On my comfortable bed,
I stare at the ceiling
Until I am fed
Up with thinking and feeling.

Two Hand-Rhymes for Grown-ups

1

The Shrink

Here's a head.
Here's a shrink.
Listen carefully.
What does he think?

He thinks you're crazy,
A nervous wreck.
Say, 'Thank you, doctor',
And write the cheque.

2

Publishers

Five happy publishers,
Going through a door.
One met an author
And then there were four.

Four happy publishers,
Out on a spree.
Someone had to pay the bill
And then there were three.

Three happy publishers,
Nothing much to do.
A big fat manuscript arrived
And then there were two.

Two happy publishers,
Having lots of fun.
An author won a major prize
And then there was one.

One happy publisher,
Radiant as the sun.
The winner found an agent,
And then there were none.

III

The Uncertainty of the Poet

'The Tate Gallery yesterday announced that it had paid £1 million for a Giorgio de Chirico masterpiece, The Uncertainty of the Poet. *It depicts a torso and a bunch of bananas.' (Guardian,* 2 April 1985)

I am a poet.
I am very fond of bananas.

I am bananas.
I am very fond of a poet.

I am a poet of bananas.
I am very fond,

A fond poet of 'I am, I am' –
Very bananas,

Fond of 'Am I bananas,
Am I?' – a very poet.

Bananas of a poet!
Am I fond?' Am I very?

Poet bananas! I am.
I am fond of a 'very'.

I am of very fond bananas.
Am I a poet?

Tumps

Don't ask him the time of day. He won't know it,
For he's the abstracted sort.
In fact, he's a typically useless male poet.
We'll call him a tump for short.

A tump isn't punctual or smart or efficient,
He probably can't drive a car
Or follow a map, though he's very proficient
At finding his way to the bar.

He may have great talent, and not just for writing –
For drawing, or playing the drums.
But don't let him loose on accounts – that's inviting
Disaster. A tump can't do sums.

He cannot get organized. Just watch him try it
And you'll see a frustrated man.
But some tumps (and these are the worst ones)
   deny it
And angrily tell you they can.

I used to be close to a tump who would bellow
'You think I can't add two and two!'
And get even crosser when, smiling and mellow,
I answered, 'You're quite right. I do.'

Women poets are businesslike, able,
Good drivers, and right on the ball,
And some of us still know our seven times table.
We're not like the tumps. Not at all.

Poem Composed in Santa Barbara

The poets talk. They talk a lot.
They talk of T. S. Eliot.
One is anti. One is pro.
How hard they think! How much they know!
They're happy. A cicada sings.
We women talk of other things.

The Cricketing Versions

(for Simon Rae)

'There isn't much cricket in the Cromwell play.'
     (overheard at a dinner-party)

There isn't much cricket in *Hamlet* either,
There isn't much cricket in *Lear*.
I don't think there's any in *Paradise Lost** –
I haven't a copy right here.

But I like to imagine the cricketing versions –
Laertes goes out to bat
And instead of claiming a palpable hit,
The prince gives a cry of 'Howzat!'

While elsewhere the nastier daughters of Lear
(Both women cricketers) scheme
To keep their talented younger sister
Out of the England team,

And up in the happy realms of light
When Satan is out (great catch)
His team and the winners sit down together
For sandwiches after the match.

---

* Apparently there is. 'Chaos umpire sits,/ And by decision more embroils
the fray.' *Paradise Lost*, Book II, lines 907–8.

Although there are some English writers
Who feature the red leather ball,
You could make a long list of the plays and the
  books
In which there's no cricket at all.

To be perfectly honest, I like them that way –
The absence of cricket is fine.
But if you prefer work that includes it, please note
That now there's some cricket in mine.

19th Christmas Poem

(for Nicholas Shakespeare and John Coldstream)

Christmas is coming.
The phone rings and I curse.
Literary editor.
Seasonal verse.

Big deal. Big chance
To sell them a rhyme.
They never publish poetry
Except at Christmas-time.

Christmas is coming,
Last week in September.
Can you let us have it
By the second of November?

Light and clean and printable –
You know the kind of thing.
If you want a Christmas bonus,
Now's the time to sing.

Christmas is coming.
Books of the year.
I re-read *Persuasion*,
War and Peace, King Lear.

We don't count that stuff.
It isn't what we mean.
We thought you were part
Of the literary scene.

Christmas is coming.
Better play the game.
Mother reads the *Telegraph*.
She likes to see my name.

Last year it made her
Happy as a bird
To find her elder daughter
Under Douglas Hurd.

Christmas is coming.
Here's my Christmas song –
Light and clean and printable
And forty lines long.

Dear Dial-a-Poet,
Hope it will do.
Please to pay without delay
And God bless you.

The Poet's Song

(Tune: 'The Lord Chancellor's Song' from *Iolanthe*.)

When I started to write as a very young man
(Said I to myself – said I),
I'll always produce the best work that I can
(Said I to myself – said I).
I've devoted myself to the life of the mind
And I shan't drop my standards at all, should I find
That my mortgage repayments have fallen behind
(Said I to myself – said I).

If I get a call from the BBC
(Said I to myself – said I),
I'll be pithy and terse and to hell with the fee
(Said I to myself – said I).
They pay by the minute. It wouldn't be hard
To run the stuff off by the foot or the yard
And forget it tomorrow. I'll be on my guard,
(Said I to myself – said I).

I shan't include stanzas I'm iffy about
(Said I to myself – said I),
Or use a refrain just to pad the thing out
(Said I to myself – said I).
If it's metrically wonky, I shan't send it in
And hope that the Muse will forgive me my sin
And that the producer has ears made of tin,
(Said I to myself – said I).

It's better to be conscientious and poor
(Said I to myself – said I),
All poets abide by this maxim, I'm sure
(Said I to myself – said I),
And that's why you never hear second-rate stuff,
A trifle long-winded or boring or duff
And scream at your radio set, 'That's enough!'
(Said I to myself – said I).

Note: This was written in response to a request from BBC Radio for a new poem. It has not been broadcast.

Reflections on a Royalty Statement

They've given me a number
So they will know it's me
And not some other Wendy Cope
(They publish two or three).
When I go to see them
I wear a number-plate
Or sometimes I salute and say,
'032838.'

What a lot of authors!
The digits make it clear
That publishers are busy –
You can phone them once a year
But it isn't done to grumble
If the cheque's a little late:
'Look, we've other things to think about,
032838.'

Sometimes they give a party
And all the numbers go.
'It's 027564!'
'036040!'
'Hey, have you seen 014's book?
You're right. He's second-rate.
But even so he's better than
032838.'

We're one big happy family
(My eyes are getting runny)
And, what is more, if we do well
They give us pocket-money!
Some publishers are terrible
But mine are really great.
OK? Can this go in my book? –
032838.

Pastoral

I wish I was a provincial poet,
Writing a lot about nature,
Whenever I thought about London poets,
I'd mutter darkly, 'I hate yer.'

And off I'd stomp down the wild, wild lanes
In my jeans and my wellington boots.
A provincial poet doesn't need lipstick
Or tights or respectable suits –

The clutter of urban life. How wonderful
Just to discard it all
And spend one's time communing with everything,
Perched on a dry-stone wall.

And after a busy day communing
To amble back home for a bite,
Then go to the pub with some real people,
Who manage twelve pints in a night,

Which helps them get through the provincial
    evenings
Without too much boredom or pain.
Real people, as solid and ruddy and calm
As a London bus in the rain!

Some day I'll go and live in the country
And many a notebook I'll fill
With keen observations of animals (mostly
The dead ones because they keep still).

Dead sheep and squashed rabbits. Oh, how I shall
    love it.
My face will be peaceful and brown
And shining with love for all of creation,
Excepting those poets in town.

An Argument with Wordsworth

'Poetry . . . takes its origin from emotion recollected in tranquillity'
(Preface to the *Lyrical Ballads*)

People are always quoting that and all of them seem
   to agree
And it's probably most unwise to admit that it's
   different for me.
I have emotion – no one who knows me could fail to
   detect it –
But there's a serious shortage of tranquillity in
   which to recollect it.
So this is my contribution to the theoretical debate:
Sometimes poetry is emotion recollected in a highly
   emotional state.

Variation on Belloc's 'Fatigue'

I hardly ever tire of love or rhyme –
That's why I'm poor and have a rotten time.

IV

Does She Like Word-Games?

She likes sonnets but she doesn't like poems.
She doesn't like sestinas or whisky.
No, she doesn't like limericks either, or water, or
    television or cats.

She likes sweets but she doesn't like eating.
She likes apples too.

She likes Schumann but she doesn't like Stravinsky.
She's fond of jazz and piccolos.
She dislikes songs.

She has a warm regard for Russian dancers,
Spanish jugglers, little people,
Especially if they're green.

She likes especially as well. And as well
For that matter. And for that matter.
She can't stand Shakespeare.

Among her favourites are spelling bees,
Football, the Book of Common Prayer.
And there are great loves –
James Russell Lowell, the Mississippi.

She likes sonnets but she doesn't like the sky.

She doesn't like repetition.
She doesn't like repetition.

She doesn't like endings.

Magnetic

i spell it out on this fridge door
you are so wonderful
i even like th way you snor

Variation on a Lennon and McCartney Song

Love, love, love,
Love, love, love,
Love, love, love,
Dooby doo dooby doo,
All you need is love,
Dooby dooby doo,
All you need is love,
Dooby dooby doo,
All you need is love, love
Or, failing that, alcohol.

English Weather

January's grey and slushy,
February's chill and drear,
March is wild and wet and windy,
April seldom brings much cheer.
In May, a day or two of sunshine,
Three or four in June, perhaps.
July is usually filthy,
August skies are open taps.
In September things start dying,
Then comes cold October mist.
November we make plans to spend
The best part of December pissed.

From Strugnell Lunaire

The silver moon pours down her light.
I drink it in with thirsty eyes.
I'd rather have another pint of lager
But all the pubs are closed.
The poet must drink deep of life
To find poetic ecstasy.
The silver moon pours down her light.
I drink it in with thirsty eyes.
Tonight I am intoxicated
And every night it is the same.
I wander down the beauteous High Street
And, if the weather isn't cloudy,
The silver moon pours down her light.

the homeless hammer

I *furious objects*

the sick umbrella underneath the council chamber
and a cow in the washbasin
I rage, a cushion in captivity
the teapot will not break its bonds

II *second sight in Brockwell Park*

my toenails listen
to the soggy grass
mankind – a wind-tossed ice-cream wrapper
life – a melancholy bus
I walk, I have these visions
and they are really quite depressing

III *solitary beer-mat*

the clock has lost its knitting, it needs a woman
eyes in the paving-stones are weeping
to see pink elephants in Norwood Road

Ahead of My Time

poems for musical performance
by Jason Strugnell

Clouds

Sprinkle the air around you
with short, quiet sounds

Make more and more raindrops
until your co-players

are drenched

Let the intervals between sounds
grow longer

When you have finished raining
hold still
Loom

Perplexity

Gaze into the eyes
of a co-player

At irregular intervals
scratch your head

Weltschmerz

Play and/or sing

extremely long quiet sounds

When the tedium
has become unbearable

scream

Quartet for Four Beer-drinkers

From your pint glass
take a swig of beer
whenever you feel like it

When you are not actually drinking
strike your glass
with an implement

sometimes quietly
sometimes loudly

Let there be silences between your attacks

Continue
until all four glasses are empty

Strugnell's Christian Songs

1
(to the tune *Daisy Bell*)

Jesus, Jesus! Who is on Jesus' side?
Wear His colours, sing out His name with pride!
Supporters of His eleven
Are sure to get to Heaven.
Up in the sky, while others fry,
We'll be winners who never died!

Jesus came to work with me today.
He kept me calm and happy all the way.
He didn't make a fuss
About the crowded bus
Or moan about conditions, hours and pay.

Jesus came to work, He came along.
I carried out my duties with a song.
I went the extra mile
And wore a Christian smile –
The smile that says, 'I know I can't be wrong.'

Jesus came to work, He came to lunch
With me and Tony and the usual bunch.
I bought a round of beers
And said, 'To Jesus. Cheers!'
And Tony laughed and, Lord, that was the crunch.

Jesus told me, 'Turn the other cheek.'
And so I did, but first I had to speak.
I muttered 'Just you wait
Till you get to Heaven's gate,
You jerk.' Then I went back to being meek.

Jesus came to work, my feet were swift,
My spirits kept on soaring like the lift.
Being saved is bliss –
It helps me write like this.
Thank you, Lord, for my poetic gift.

3

for Fraser Steel

When I went out shopping,
I said a little prayer:
'Jesus, help me park the car
For you are everywhere.'

Jesus, in His goodness and grace,
Jesus found me a parking space
In a very convenient place.
Sound the horn and praise Him!

His eternal car-park
Is hidden from our eyes.
Trust in Him and you will have
A space beyond the skies.

Jesus, in His goodness and grace,
Wants to find you a parking space.
Ask Him now to reserve a place.
Sound the horn and praise Him!

V

Faint Praise

Size isn't everything. It's what you do
That matters, darling, and you do quite well
In some respects. Credit where credit's due –
You work, you're literate, you rarely smell.
Small men can be aggressive, people say,
But you are often genial and kind,
As long as you can have things all your way
And I comply, and do not speak my mind.
You look all right. I've never been disgusted
By paunchiness. Who wants some skinny youth?
My friends have warned me that you can't be trusted
But I protest I've heard you tell the truth.
Nobody's perfect. Now and then, my pet,
You're almost human. You could make it yet.

Men and Their Boring Arguments

One man on his own can be quite good fun
But don't go drinking with two –
They'll probably have an argument
And take no notice of you.

What makes men so tedious
Is the need to show off and compete.
They'll bore you to death for hours and hours
Before they'll admit defeat.

It often happens at dinner-parties
Where brother disputes with brother
And we can't even talk among ourselves
Because we're not next to each other.

Some men like to argue with women –
Don't give them a chance to begin.
You won't be allowed to change the subject
Until you have given in.

A man with the bit between his teeth
Will keep you up half the night
And the only way to get some sleep
Is to say, 'I expect you're right.'

I expect you're right, my dearest love.
I expect you're right, my friend.
These boring arguments make no difference
To anything in the end.

I Worry

I worry about you –
So long since we spoke.
Love, are you downhearted,
Dispirited, broke?

I worry about you.
I can't sleep at night.
Are you sad? Are you lonely?
Or are you all right?

They say that men suffer,
As badly, as long.
I worry, I worry,
In case they are wrong.

Two Cures for Love

1 Don't see him. Don't phone or write a letter.
2 The easy way: get to know him better.

Advice to Young Women

When you're a spinster of forty,
You're reduced to considering bids
From husbands inclined to be naughty
And divorcés obsessed with their kids.

So perhaps you should wed in a hurry,
But that has its drawbacks as well.
The answer? There's no need to worry –
Whatever you do, life is hell.

Exchange of Letters

'Man who is a serious novel would like to hear from a woman who is a poem' (classified advertisement, *New York Review of Books*)

Dear Serious Novel,

I am a terse, assured lyric with impeccable rhythmic flow, some apt and original metaphors, and a music that is all my own. Some people say I am beautiful.

My vital statistics are eighteen lines, divided into three-line stanzas, with an average of four words per line.

My first husband was a cheap romance; the second was *Wisden's Cricketers' Almanac*. Most of the men I meet nowadays are autobiographies, but a substantial minority are books about photography or trains.

I have always hoped for a relationship with an upmarket work of fiction. Please write and tell me more about yourself.

Yours intensely,
Song of the First Snowdrop

Dear Song of the First Snowdrop,

Many thanks for your letter. You sound like just the kind of poem I am hoping to find. I've always preferred short, lyrical women to the kind who go on for page after page.

I am an important 150,000 word comment on the dreams and dilemmas of twentieth-century Man. It took six years to attain my present weight and stature but all the twenty-seven publishers I have so far approached have failed to understand me. I have my share of sex and violence and a very good joke in chapter nine, but to no avail. I am sustained by the belief that I am ahead of my time.

Let's meet as soon as possible. I am longing for you to read me from cover to cover and get to know my every word.

> Yours impatiently,
> Death of the Zeitgeist

So Much Depends

'And another thing: I gave in far too easily over William Carlos Williams.'

I can't remember what you said about him.
Was it thumbs down or the big hurrah?
When it comes to William Carlos Williams,
I've no idea what your opinions are.

I argued with you? That seems most unlikely.
I may have looked attentive for a while.
I've searched my head for William Carlos Williams
And there is very little in the file.

I'll fight with you about important issues
Like who should buy the bread or clean the sink
But when it comes to William Carlos Williams,
Dearest, I really don't mind what you think.

Yes, mutter darkly, 'Well, perhaps you ought to,'
And fire offensive weapons from those eyes.
When it comes to William Carlos Williams,
It won't do any good. I will not rise.

Noises in the Night

Why are men so good at sleeping?
Is it just the drink?
While we're tossing, turning, weeping,
Why are they so good at sleeping?
Snoring, whistling, grunting, beeping –
No one else can get a wink.
Why are men so good at sleeping?
Is it just the drink?

Another Christmas Poem

Bloody Christmas, here again.
Let us raise a loving cup:
Peace on earth, goodwill to men,
And make them do the washing-up.

VI

Letter

Alone too much this week,
I'm in my poet mode –
Awake at half past five and writing,
Dozing on the sofa-bed by ten.

You're there, of course, my absent angel,
But for once we don't make love
Or even talk. You have been working
In another room and then

You come in, carrying a blanket,
And cover me while I'm asleep.
It's cold today. I need the blanket.
You do it over and over again.

Favourite

When they ask me, 'Who's your favourite poet?'
I'd better not mention you,
Though you certainly are my favourite poet
And I like your poems too.

Nine-line Triolet

Here's a fine mess we got ourselves into,
My angel, my darling, true love of my heart
Etcetera. Must stop it but I can't begin to.
Here's a fine mess we got ourselves into –
Both in a spin with nowhere to spin to,
Bound by the old rules in life and in art.
Here's a fine mess we got ourselves into,
(I'll curse every rule in the book as we part)
My angel, my darling, true love of my heart.

On a Country Bus

The fat boy in the seat across the aisle
Is reading *Dragons of Autumn Twilight Volume One*
And listening to something dreadful on his Walkman.
Sometimes I wish I needed books and music
More than I do. Today I don't need anything –
I didn't want my lunch. And, more remarkable,
I feel quite tolerant about the tinny buzzing
From his earphones. I shall just sit back
And think about the things you say and do
And nothing else. The journey takes almost an hour.

After the Lunch

On Waterloo Bridge, where we said our goodbyes,
The weather conditions bring tears to my eyes.
I wipe them away with a black woolly glove
And try not to notice I've fallen in love.

On Waterloo Bridge I am trying to think:
This is nothing. You're high on the charm and the drink.
But the juke-box inside me is playing a song
That says something different. And when was it
   wrong?

On Waterloo Bridge with the wind in my hair
I am tempted to skip. *You're a fool.* I don't care.
The head does its best but the heart is the boss –
I admit it before I am halfway across.

In the Rhine Valley

Die Farben der Bäume sind schön
And the sky's and the river's blue-greys
And the *Burg,* almost lost in the haze.

You're patient. You help me to learn
And you smile as I practise the phrase,
'Die Farben der Bäume sind schön.'

October. The year's on the turn –
It will take us our separate ways
But the sun shines. And we have two days.
Die Farben der Bäume sind schön.

New Season

No coats today. Buds bulge on chestnut trees,
and on the doorstep of a big, old house
a young man stands and plays his flute.

I watch the silver notes fly up
and circle in blue sky above the traffic,
travelling where they will.

And suddenly this paving-stone
midway between my front door and the bus stop
is a starting-point.

From here I can go anywhere I choose.

Legacy

She left two Premium Bonds
And what remained of that week's pension,
Her clothes, photographs, and china ornaments
We'd given her as children.

Also the crocheted mats
She made as wedding presents,
Babies' shawls, the suit
My teddy bear still wears,
And fifty pairs of woolly socks
In drawers all over England.

Names

She was Eliza for a few weeks
When she was a baby –
Eliza Lily. Soon it changed to Lil.

Later she was Miss Steward in the baker's shop
And then 'my love', 'my darling', Mother.

Widowed at thirty, she went back to work
As Mrs Hand. Her daughter grew up,
Married and gave birth.

Now she was Nanna. 'Everybody
Calls me Nanna,' she would say to visitors.
And so they did – friends, tradesmen, the doctor.

In the geriatric ward
They used the patients' Christian names.
'Lil,' we said, 'or Nanna,'
But it wasn't in her file
And for those last bewildered weeks
She was Eliza once again.

For My Sister, Emigrating

You've left with me
the things you couldn't take
or bear to give away –
books, records and a biscuit-tin
that Nanna gave you.

It's old and dirty
and the lid won't fit.
Standing in a corner of my room,
quite useless, it's as touching
as a once loved toy.

Yes, sentimental now –
but if you'd stayed,
we would have quarrelled
just the same as ever,
found excuses not to phone.

We never learn. We've grown up
struggling, frightened
that the family would drown us,
only giving in to love
when someone's dead or gone.

Leaving

(for Dick and Afkham)

Next summer? The summer after?
With luck we've a few more years
Of sunshine and drinking and laughter
And airports and goodbyes and tears.